Grow from Life's Yeses, Nos, and Waits

Daily Inspirational Gift Messages

Grow from Life's Yeses, Nos, and Waits

Daily Inspirational Gift Messages

Elizabeth George
Illustrations by L. Samuels

Valued Educational Services, LLC

Published first in 2018 by Valued Educational Services, LLC
5520 Lyndon B. Johnson Freeway, Suite 365
Dallas, Texas 75240
e-mail: drmves@att.net
www.globalves.com

Grow from Life's Yeses, Nos, and Waits: Daily Inspirational Gift Messages/
Elizabeth George.

Issued in print and electronic formats:
ISBN 978-1-7322846-2-3
eBook ISBN 978-1-7322846-3-0

Cover design and book illustrations © L. Samuels

Printed and bound in the United States of America
TXu002102636 / 2018-08-22

Quantity sales: Special discount are available on quantity purchases by
corporations, associations, and others. For more detail, contact the publisher
at the address above.

To:

The joy of friendships and the strength
of positive relationships.

Table of Contents

Table of Contents

Introduction

There is a distinct place of harmony and rest that exists for you. In this place you can experience and share the best of who you are, and so I write with the aim of helping you find and live in your comfort zone.

Grow from Life's Yeses, Nos, and Waits is written to help you process uncertainties and difficulties and for you to expect and welcome positive and important victories. It is an inspirational read that invites you to take time to know who you are and embrace yourself.

My idea for this book, first, is to have a conversation with you. Secondly, I thought of certain lessons I would like to share by using one word that develops into a daily gem. For example, the word "Today" inspired the daily gem—"Give today your best effort, and tomorrow will take care of itself".

Each gem prompts you to consider and think about how

you process your thoughts and make decisions. The word and gem connect to a daily read, which I call your "gift message". It is my hope that each gift message is useful and lasting.

Grow from Life's Yeses, Nos, and Waits is the first of three conversational series that is thought-provoking and encourages you to discover and grow. This book includes 31 words that are not arranged in any particular order, because my intent is for you to decide which daily read is most suited for you on any particular day or days.

The significance of the number 31 is that it represents any of the longest months in the year. This ensures that for each day, in any month, you can find a gem and its related gift message that compliment or improve your outlook.

There is a self-actualization I endeavor for you to derive and achieve. Be mindful of your individual process as you read. First, decide to be more patient and forgiving to yourself. Then, realize that acknowledging and understanding who you are will allow you to enjoy the feats of your better moments and boost your ability to work through challenges. As you read and reflect, remain conscious of how you can conserve and preserve your energy and appreciate your values.

It is important to become informed about what and who

works for you and around you and which cause or group you decide to join or support. These decisions will help fuel your energy source and storage.

Seek to develop and sharpen awareness and know that transformation is realized beyond a moment. Transformation is achieved along a continuum.

The words, gems, and gift messages create an arc of hope for you to take steps in making decisions, allowing you to live calmly with knowledge and without fear of time—past, present, or future.

Each reading is meant to be self-interactive, in that you should become introspective. Give yourself the time to clarify your thoughts, reflect, and examine your practices.

You should also find that you will want to discuss your thoughts and ideas because a discovery gains value when it is shared and used. A lesson is not a lesson unless it is taught, learned, and put into action.

∝ Today ∝

Give today your best effort, and tomorrow will take care of itself.

If every day you make the decision to be and do the best you can, rest assured you have already begun laying the foundation for your tomorrow.

Endeavor to have realistic expectations so that you can feel satisfied and accomplished, even if all your "to dos" are not complete.

Often times, we plan too much in our days and become disappointed or self-defeated when we do not meet these goals. A useful approach is to prioritize activities with tasks that are essential and those you can actually accomplish in a day.

Sometimes all it takes is a pause, being thoughtful about your energy, and acknowledging that time cannot be controlled.

Leave room in your day to: 1) respond to the unforeseen instead of reacting; and 2) receive favors as you remain wise to avoid careless slights to gifts that might not recur in your future.

Though you might not have full knowledge of your past or ideas for your future, do not leave your present only to fortuitous occurrences. Have your say. Create and practice individual approaches to stay in tune.

As you mature in directing your days, each day will be made more durable from the strides of yesterdays, and you will become less concerned about your tomorrows.

It is also important not to be overwhelmed with tasks, chores, and deadlines. Include moments of calm, rest, or laughter.

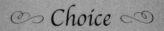

Many important facts about us are inherited and cultural, but choice is uniquely in our domain.

Do not say, "I cannot" or "I have to". Instead say, "I choose" because you are aware of who you are, what you will incorporate in your life, and what you will not tolerate.

My pursuit for wisdom and discernment has informed me that when we choose to accept our originality and allow ourselves the freedom to thrive, we acquire an awareness that helps us understand our purpose.

In understanding our purpose, it becomes easier to make choices that permit us to realize and live in the fulfillment of our imagination and creativity.

Identify and determine your boundaries, and know how to compromise without compromising yourself. Reflect, consider, and make the choice to choose.

ℰ∽ Voice ∾℘

Letting your voice be heard is knowing when to be silent.

Our voices make us part of conversations and allow us to be recognized. Be it through speaking, writing, or sign language, there is energy in our voices that individualizes each of us.

Beyond the words used, your voice communicates your stances and ideas. And so it is like a fingerprint that uniquely identifies and separates you from all others.

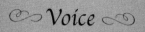

By its very volume, intonation, or frequency, your voice informs listeners of your emotions, disposition, and thoughts. It shares your positions on issues.

The voice holds artistic attributes, like a painting or musical instrument; it can soothe, provoke, or even awaken the imagination. Listen to your voice and hear what it shares. Is it conveying what you intend? Be your most avid listener.

7

❧ Perceptions ❧

How you perceive your life is how you will live.

What you derive from life is directly determined and shaped by your perceptions. If you perceive life to be positive, you will likely think and make decisions that are positive. Moreover, the act of thinking positively adds joy to your moments and hence your existence.

It is often said that how you are perceived by others is partly true. But, is this always the case? Without their knowledge of who you are or themselves, what is considered a perception is without merit and does not exist, unless you give it life.

When a person expresses an opinion of you, it is wise to consider what is being said. However, do not gloss over the reality of considering, as well, his/her intentions. In this moment, you may learn more about the speaker and less about who they think you are. Actually, you may realize that what is being said is a person's "self-projection".

Think of what you learn about those who spend their time sharing their opinions of others as compared to what you learn from people who share information about themselves.

When there is incongruence between how you perceive yourself and an individual's opinion of you, objectively examine the differences that exist.

It is your perception of yourself that is most important.

❧ Words ❧

Words are powerful; they will define and inform others about you.

Use positive words to describe yourself and act accordingly. Do you listen to how you describe yourself to others? Consider the words used to describe yourself, whether openly or privately.

Your messaging will influence your actions and how others conceive who you are. Think of words as self-branding in an advertising campaign of your life.

It is equally important how you describe others. Regardless of how you think or feel about a person, be thoughtful and wise when speaking of others, especially when they are not in your presence or have an opportunity to respond.

How you speak and what you say is also a reflection of yourself. Do not be stained or strained by the less than flattering words you choose to say about another person. Even in moments when you believe the words are well-suited to describe another, never forget that the words you use are self-branding.

Through words, you have the opportunity to launch your best life campaign. Know what you desire and deserve, and be willing to advocate for yourself.

You are your best agent.

❧ *Rejections* ❧

Acceptance of yourself will bring you relief.

When you have been rejected by someone you love, care about, or depend upon— may it be a friend, parent, family member, or a special someone— it is likely that you will feel a mix or range of emotions that can be complicated to process and resolve. Any one or a combination of these emotions is quite real, and so I decided to focus on understanding the origin.

I have concluded that there is some level of ownership or meaning you have attached to the source of the rejection, and therefore it is within your will to work through the emotions. Consider for a moment, two questions— do you have control over a person's words or actions? Also, why would you allow someone to be the source of prolonged emotions that are not beneficial?

The answer to the first question is definitely no. Also, you will begin answering the second question if you accept at the very least some ownership of your feelings. The process of understanding and working through your emotions may take some time, but it will be worthwhile. Give yourself the time to find the answers. If you need help, take steps to seek the help you need.

Please note that these feelings have very little to do with being rejected by someone who is not deserving of your love and care. In part or in whole, it is more about an unrealized idea at a particular time. It is the idea of who you thought the person was or should have been to you that influenced the interactions between you and this person and created your expectations of the relationship.

Often we create images or personifications based on our ideas of who we want a person to be. We then hold a false belief that the person whom we thought loved or cared about us fits the profile and embodies the ideas and ideals we hold dearly. In such instances, it is more about what we hold dearly and less about the person that is now the catalyst for the surfaced emotions.

Take a moment to think and question the idea you held about what such a person would/should have contributed or shared in your life. Notice you still have your idea even though the particular person has moved on.

When you experience a rejection, is it the person you miss experiencing or is it the idea of whom you thought the person to be that you yearn for? Seriously consider this question, because just maybe this process of consideration could bring about an admission that provides you a different realization of the person and even yourself.

You may find that a renewed assessment of the person and yourself will ease you into an acceptance of the experience. For after all, there is value to be gained from this experience, which could help transport you from rejection to recognition and reveal the origin of your emotions.

When a person turns away from you or seems to turn away, this may have little or nothing to do with you. Frequently, what may seem to be an affront towards you is that person's inability to deal or respond to simple virtues of strength, talent, or truth that exists within or about you.

Please do not attribute another's inability onto you. Each person needs to grow at his/her own pace. Also, consider if what you may have perceived as a rejection could have been another's inability to manage his/her life. Their actions or words could have been based on a personal decision irrespective of you or anyone else.

Realize that your future will be made better without someone who is incapable of receiving and accepting you or does not embody the ideas or ideals you seek in a person with whom you desire a particular relationship. Just maybe the person has made a decision for the betterment of his/herself.

Regardless, discomforted emotions are difficult. There is no unique or general response to each rejection since most often they occur in personal or close relationships, with specific facts and occurrences.

This is what I can share. Experience your emotions and make the choice not to tarry in a place that does not progress your ideas and ideals. Find the strength to transition or pivot into a thinking place with the resolute knowledge that you are worthwhile and worthy of your ideas and ideals.

Find the space in which you will be in acceptance of yourself. Acceptance of yourself will help you to emerge and grow from the experience of a rejection. The emotions will fade if you take the time to identify the origin and develop an approach to work through relationship(s) that end, and find closure for yourself.

Take actions to surround yourself with positive people who have the ability to give and receive. Prosper in happiness by engaging in activities you enjoy, and seek to learn more about yourself.

Awareness

Being aware allows you to clearly hear your thoughts.

In your daily interactions, practice being attentive to your thoughts, spoken words, silences, and responses. Being aware of people, places, and things can help you identify what triggers your discomforts and the signals that make you feel at ease.

Awareness helps you better assess which actions provide desired results and the option to build on those moments and gains. Being aware can also help sustain your health and safety. A decision to go or stay or a simple yes or no can change the trajectory of your life.

Pause for a moment and reflect. It is first being aware of who you are that determines in those decisive moments how you will respond. When you are aware, you will be self-directed and guided by decisions to create positive actions.

As your awareness matures, you will operate from a vantage of action rather than reaction— proactive versus reactive. As well, you will be the subject in your story that is promoted by you and not the object in a tale of others.

ℰℴ Responsibility ℰℴ

Ownership of your thoughts, words, and actions are essential.

Part of being responsible is identifying who you are, understanding the world in which you exist, knowing how to interact, and navigating your journey.

As an individual living amongst several different peoples, ideas, and places, you have a responsibility to devise a strategy to co-exist. Learning your best fit within our dynamic ecosystem of cultures, philosophies, and shifting social constructs is your responsibility.

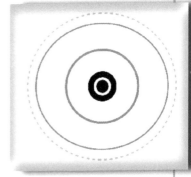

It can, for example, be as simple as being solitary, having many associations and friends, or deciding to exist somewhere else along this spectrum.

A tool that I use, actually and metaphorically, is to construct what I call, "Concentric Circles of My Life". My most important people, ideas, and places are positioned on the innermost circle that is closest to the origin of my circles— me.

I keep building circles of ideas, places, and people around me with the willingness to rearrange my construction when I derive new information.

You are responsible for constructing a tool or an approach to help you determine how to live as an individual and co-exist within our one world.

What decisions have you made about who, why, where, and the importance each has in your life?

❧ Strengths ❧

Strive to be guided by your strengths and not controlled by your weaknesses.

Strengths and weaknesses are built through our thoughts and fueled by how we are or have been impacted by external influences.

The reasons for how and why we convert certain thoughts into actions can be manifestations of either our strengths or weaknesses.

Equally, the conversion of our thoughts into actions can be explained as an aggregate or partial composition of our strengths and weaknesses.

Albeit the varied reasons why you act, it helps to know your strengths and weaknesses. There are moments when you may act as either an expression of your strengths or your weaknesses, which could reverberate beyond the turn of a head because of its exceptional nature or odd impact.

Your actions could change your life's compass and take you to unimaginable heights. Or the unfortunate alternative is also true. Let it not be you who is surprised by your strengths or weaknesses, because you have not taken the time to understand your personal dimensions and hence the actions they could manifest.

No one knows or should know your strengths and weaknesses better than you. It is up to each of us to be conscious of these facts and take note of what situations and experiences foster our strengths and help us make decisions that uplift the best of who we are and aspire to be.

My decision has been to redefine my weaknesses and think of them more as limitations. I also believe there is no need for me to promote or announce my limitations. I, thereby, work to identify and minimize the sources that precipitate my limitations, as I take on opportunities to bolster my strengths. Hold fast to your strengths and remain conscious of your weaknesses.

Recognize that our weaknesses are the equipoise for our strengths; in that they are not meant to diminish us, but are instead purposed to focus us on what keeps us strong—our strengths.

❦ Truth ❧

Truth solicits truth.

To discern and understand your interactions, you should endeavor to establish and share the truth about yourself. When you stand in your truth, you are standing in your principles and possibilities. In this space, you will be best able to discover and accomplish.

When I converse or participate in discourses with an open mind, I contribute and say exactly what I think or believe. I remain in tune to all forms of responses, from the unspoken to the spoken words, and those that can only be surmised through the expressions of the face or body.

There are times when some will leave the conversation or might decide not to engage ever again. This might be disheartening, but wouldn't you prefer to know who accepts you and who does not? After all, it is impossible for your opinions and ideas to be accepted by all when people have different dispositions, opinions, values, etc.

Now, just for a moment, ponder the alternative. Should you or I speak and act based on what is generally expected, how can we know if what is reciprocated is truth?

Much too often people are not taken at their words and actions. There is the misguided practice of making assumptions or conclusions when there are no justifications supported by body language, tone, or a conflicting emotion. This practice seems challenging and arduous when it should be so easy to say exactly what is meant, with the comfort that the listener will accurately interpret your message.

When you are engaged in dialogue, and doubts should arise, follow-up with questions and listen more closely. Seek to share and receive the truth in order to gain common understanding.

Take for instance you meet someone and through actions and words you have decided to develop a relationship. How long can either of you act or speak just to be liked or nice? When I was in my early teens, I made the decision that the best character I would be in the theater of life is me. This decision revealed, amazingly at an early age, who is who— friends, acquaintances, and others.

Throughout my life when I meet people, by being myself, I can quickly determine who will be a friend, acquaintance, or other. These interactions have made me ever so determined to be seen truly as I am. The refreshing result is that I have more time to share and give to the people with whom I am compatible.

Regardless of your age, are you being true, especially when and where it matters? May it be the small moments or when you have an experience of great importance, acknowledge why and be willing to consider if the experience was consistent with the standards and stances you hold as true.

Do not wait until it is too late to discover and share who you are. Knowing and living your truth will help you to better understand the whys and wherefores of your life journey.

❧ Alignment ❧

Think-Decide-Act

When your thoughts and actions are aligned, you will experience a peace of mind that makes it less likely for you to be staggered or disquieted by your outcomes.

Realize that speech is also an action, and therefore, your words and thoughts should align. No one knows your thoughts until you speak or engage in some other form of action.

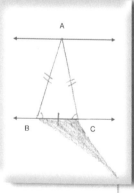

Importantly, you should not be confused or alarmed by your own actions. It is therefore necessary for your thoughts, decisions, and actions to be in harmony in order to support and present consistency and reliability.

The actions we impart are not meant only for onlookers. Review the composition of your actions and the messages you convey and teach yourself. Self-assessment of our outputs and dispositions are necessary for our alignment and can help us determine if our actions are aligned with our thinking.

The approach I take is to remain alert to my thoughts and actions in order to secure my overall synchronization. At first it may seem like work, and maybe it is, but being perceptive to my thoughts prepares me for being attentive to my life.

I literally see patterns and information that construct lessons, which teach me about my actions. These lessons enlighten my thinking and help me to make adjustments when necessary. Whenever an experience does not equate or fit within my paradigm, I evaluate and reprocess the successions of my thoughts, decisions, and actions to understand the reason for the disconnection.

You must identify and practice what it takes to maintain your base so that you can design and build your life to attain and experience your apex.

You can begin by evaluating your thoughts. Next, remain open and willing to realign and refine your decision-making process. Understand and note your practices that present preferred interpretations of yourself. Consider how to translate practical plans into your daily living to achieve intended and positive outcomes.

It is essential that we remain conscious about our thinking, decision-making processes, and the contributions or consequences of our actions.

∞ Confidence ∞

Embrace your personal rhythm and operate with assurance.

When norms, trends, or groups attempt to diminish you, do not despair. Let the beauty of your spirit transcend these attempts. Do not become part of a collective voice that attempts to diminish who you are.

I would be the first to say that I enjoy my profession and the amenities of life. I also acknowledge value in the professions and vocations of others and do recognize how they benefit society, including me.

At the same time, however, we are so much more than a profession, income strata, and what we naturally look like. The material and superficial list is much too long and at the same time temporal. And thus, we should not become burdened or worried about the relative nature of our existence.

On this conversation of confidence, I believe there are several circumstances that help to build or erode an individual's confidence. Also, there is no generic approach to building confidence.

What I know and can share about confidence is that when you know you have done well, do not wait for someone to congratulate you. Be able to recognize your contributions and values and congratulate yourself. Give yourself a kiss of joy and a hug of warmth. Tell yourself you are here for a reason, you matter, and you are determined to flourish in your best self.

Speak with meaning because you have invested in yourself and have obtained the knowledge that has prepared you to engage in productive conversations.

Find your stride of life and feel the energy you experience in your personal rhythm. You will smile naturally even when you are not consciously thinking of smiling. This smile I speak of is the radiance of your essence. When you smile from within, it transcends as one of the most endearing expressions of confidence and provides you the solace to know when to say yes or no.

Do not wait another moment to act in a manner that will assist you in building, restoring, and retaining your confidence so that you will operate with assurance.

❦ Wants and Desires ❦

Make sure your wants and desires are uniquely yours.

The media streams outputs that cannot be ignored for its hype and emphasis of what is expected, what others are doing, and what is trending. However, especially for the very important decisions in your life, it is imperative that you are the originator of your wants and desires. If not, you could find yourself in a quagmire of spiraling confusion.

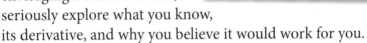

You must examine how, when, and if certain aspects or concepts of life will work for you— just you. When envisaging a want or desire, seriously explore what you know, its derivative, and why you believe it would work for you.

For instance, choose a <u>profession</u> or <u>trade</u> because you know that there is something within you or about you that will cause you to enjoy showing up each day to participate and contribute your talents and skills.

Choose a <u>life-mate</u> because you are a person who is caring, likes to share, is capable of compromising, and forgiving. Make this decision when you are ready to love and be loved by someone who knows you as you are and whom you have taken the time to know.

Have <u>children</u> because you know you will be a good provider, advocate, and protector. Inquire of yourself if you have what it takes or are willing to learn and know how to be attentive. Make sure who you choose to be your children's parent is befitting to be a parent. It is equally important that other people you bring around your children are positive examples of what you endeavor to teach them.

Often, what may work well or seems to be fantastic for another person could be burdensome for you. Do not mimic another's life and miss the opportunity of experiencing yours!

Hone your own wants and desires.

❧ Time ❧

Life requires stamina and willpower that you build over time.

Take the time you need to build your life muscles in order to plan and execute strategies for your successes. Live, plan, and make decisions for you and about yourself. Also, appreciate the value of time when choosing people to include in your life. Ease into your moments without haste, and go at your pace.

We each have different amounts of time, so do not spend it comparing yourself with others or despairing about what you do not have or who is not in your life.

Welcome what you have and learn to experience the people or places that surround you in each phase of your life. Each opportunity to learn and share, used well, prepares us for the next. There is, therefore, an undeniable value that we must seek to harness from our present.

We cannot borrow time. We cannot make or provide a loan of time. We cannot barter time. In any one moment, we cannot account for how much time we have, except the knowledge of the now.

Time is indeed a unique resource; it is to be treasured.

Facades

Who are you?

Pause, and think for a moment. Are you wearing a mask?

Remove the mask from whom you think you are, ought to be, or from what people say you are. Define yourself through the authenticity of the person you are.

With a thoughtful mind, be willing to think, speak, and write about yourself with an insightful account.

Embrace yourself in this moment of your actuality. Going forward, let your actions reflect the best of who you are while working each day to become a better person.

How can you expect to be accepted or received by another person if you do not know who you are? At your very core, you should have an accurate knowledge and a correct sense of yourself.

Discover and live your authentic self. Knowledge of yourself will provide you with better lenses for seeing and understanding.

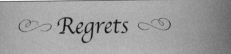

Regrets

Regrets are reminders that we are human and far from being perfect.

Whatever the reason or cause for feeling regretful, mostly likely it is an inaction or completed action that is associated with your past, but your thoughts and emotions keep it alive in your present. How do you reconcile the past to make the most of your now?

Regrets cause us to look back, and so I suggest that when you use present moments to reflect, make sure your introspection is meaningful.

You can, little by little, reconcile the regret by being fair to yourself as you acknowledge your limitations, knowledge, and strengths then as compared to now. Quite likely, your approach to processing decisions has gained new or different perspectives. Maybe you are more aware of the limitations of your actions and their impacts or outcomes.

Explore the reasons for your regrets and allow yourself to ask the whys. Write your questions and responses. Continue this process until you come to a natural pause and then continue reading this gift message.

Feeling regretful is an indication that you have experienced a shift in one or more areas of your thinking or you have gained a different insight into your decisions and actions.

At this point, you should pause again from reading and use the questions and responses to examine your life's ledger and allocate the credits you deserve. You can develop your own approach that works for you, but a simple approach I will offer is to make two columns, respectively for what I call, "life-credits (+)" and "life-debits (-)".

Do not focus solely on the debits, without including your credits. It is the likely scenario that the debits of your past are no longer recurring, but your thoughts of the past create discrepancies between then and now.

When you are no longer thinking or acting in the ways of your past that appear on the debit side of your ledger, these debits can now become zeros (0). Therefore, you must follow through with the summation to find closure and reconciliation.

Within this space of regret, there exists a kernel of new awareness that you must bring to surface above the feelings of regret. For indeed, you have assessed the past to know that your previous stance does not equate with your present position.

The next step is to recognize your transformation. Maybe it is for you to forgive yourself, ask another for forgiveness, or simply recognize the past as it was and cherish your present.

With honest examination and reconciliation, you will be fair to yourself and release the claims of past actions and the emotions that provide little or no currency for growth. Sometimes we just did not know or could not have perceived— this is being human.

When you recall and admit the past, privately or openly, place it in its correct context; you are now at a different juncture and your reconciliation of the past will equip you for the present.

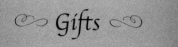

Gifts

The greatest gifts...

If you are reading this book, I will conclude that you have *life*.

This is your time; so live or strive to live your best *today*.

You have the option of *choice*; so choose with consideration.

With these gifts— life, today, and choice— I ask you to believe in yourself.

Live each day with courage and the determination to exist with thoughtfulness and purpose.

✑ Discovery ✑

Discovery is a process.

Imagine for a moment that you just developed a cure for a disease and numerous lives will be saved by your discovery. Imagine you have just designed the next social construct that will allow humans to co-exist more harmoniously. Exist for a moment or two in this space of your imagination.

For example, think of those who have gone before us whose discoveries have made it possible for us, in less than a day, to travel across continents.

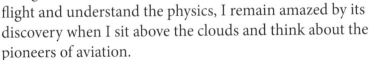

It seems such an everyday occurrence, but as much as I have thought about the invention of flight and understand the physics, I remain amazed by its discovery when I sit above the clouds and think about the pioneers of aviation.

You or I may not have the next universal discovery, but

how can we know for sure if we do not dare to imagine and make sure we discover our purpose? At the very least, make a point to discover what each day holds for you and do something about your daily thoughts and imagination.

The thoughts and imagination you set into action may just materialize into an amazing outcome. I appeal to your sense of curiosity and ask that you make a pledge of discovery to yourself.

You can never be certain that your endeavors will mature exactly as you envisioned; what is certain is that if you do nothing, your results will be naught or even negative. You owe it to yourself to put your ideas into action so that you may explore your capabilities.

Take or make opportunities that demonstrate your skills or gifts. Define your role and know what is expected. In your process of discovery, remain attentive and seek to identify your progress and productivity. Learn to communicate your contributions.

Do not be told; instead, seek to determine what your place and purpose are in this world and in your time.

☙ Dreams ❧

Your reality can be as joyous as your most beautiful dreams.

The dreams I have while asleep are not the types of dreams I speak of in this reading. There are entire books and numerous research on dreams experienced during sleep.

What I speak of are described as our waking dreams or daydreams. However, I do not intend to have a psychological discussion on daydreams. Rather, I share a lay person's approach to daydreams— my approach.

I realized that these cheerful moments of imagination brought me moments of smiles, and then triggered for me an idea— I should memorialize these moments and work to make them true.

With effort and belief, so many of my daydreams have

come true, and I have enjoyed working to materialize others. So, I am inspired to share that you should pay attention to your dreams— they hold information about your possibilities.

When I speak of daydreams, I am focusing on the thoughts we have that can be described as the hopes and aspirations we associate with our distinctive self. As a caveat, your dreams must originate genuinely from you, about you, and without comparison.

Our personal daydreams allow us to imagine our lives blossoming into a reality that makes us feel joyful, adventurous, loved, excited, fulfilled, and accomplished.

In these moments of hope and aspiration, write your dreams down, and commit to making them a reality. Hold yourself accountable to ensure that your efforts bring about tangible outcomes.

There is no guarantee that your actuality will match your dreams. However, as long as you maintain awareness that your hopes and aspirations are possible, it has been my experience that the trying is worthwhile, and the work will not be in vain.

Keep dreaming and working; stay the course; or with new information, chart new courses.

Your hopes and aspirations are important, and I am here to say you are worthy of your best daydreams!

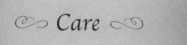

Care

Take care to evaluate your thoughts and actions.

When I think of care, I am communicating a notion of a micro-attention required in how we determine and direct our daily events. It can be easy to overlook care in our lives in the midst of the hurry and hustle of what I call, "life-pollution". Are you curious to understand the benefits of incorporating care into your daily experiences?

You will thrive when you learn how to incorporate devotion into your life. In caring for yourself, you will realize how you have become more suitable to influence positive changes that are beneficial to you. And though not by design, others will benefit as well.

Embrace your attributes in order to communicate the best of yourself, even at times when you may think it is not deserved. Know your idiosyncrasies and determine if they are factors of your nature or nurture. Further, understand what your idiosyncrasies communicate about you.

Understand that it is you and your decisions that truly matter; so step into a zone of positive thinking and take care to imbue gratification into your existence.

Be willing to self-assess. Care to realize the benefits of self-assessments and how they enable your thoughts to be dynamic and direct you to modify, correct, or fine-tune your actions.

Be gentle to yourself and take care to bring about growth that will enlighten and buttress your perceptions and expressions. In your daily pursuit, employ the practice of periodic self-reflections. Incorporating consideration into your daily life invigorates your motivation and keeps you enthusiastic about your possibilities!

⌒ Relationships ⌒

Relationships cannot be built without conversation.

If you desire to develop and build relationships, the desire must be mutual. There is no one-way relationship, and the same is true for communication.

To foster a relationship, there must be the desire to speak, thoughtfully listen, ask questions, provide honest answers, tell stories, and share ideas. Through the ease of conversation, you will come to know the level and type of relationship that is desired.

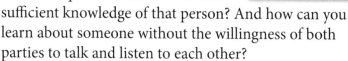

How can you want to have a relationship with someone without sufficient knowledge of that person? And how can you learn about someone without the willingness of both parties to talk and listen to each other?

In deciding who to bring into your life, you would have done yourself a great favor to develop relationships by engaging in meaningful and enjoyable conversations, as you groom your senses and embrace your inner compass.

❦ Encouragement ❦

Always be ready to dust yourself off.

I encourage you to make a positive difference in your life and the life of others.

Apply yourself so that your aptitude and abilities will appreciate.

Respect yourself and others.

Create a life path of independence as you embrace your individuality.

Work to achieve your goals so that your best ideas can become a reality.

⊗ Challenges ⊗

Challenges are the gymnastics of the human spirit.

Whether you are naturally able to sort through your challenges or it takes work, it is harnessing the belief that you will find a solution that sparks and energizes the human spirit.

To overcome your challenges, you must identify and be willing to work through them. Know as well that asking for help and accepting support, places you on a positive path.

Never be afraid to seek and find help. There are many organizations and people who are willing to help and have the requisite expertise. It is important to believe from the inception that you will emerge from the experience and overcome your challenges.

Challenges offer us opportunities to learn, grow, and contribute. If you find that you keep experiencing the same challenges, ask yourself, "What prospects or lessons am I missing, and what can be changed or done differently?" Sometimes, all it takes is changing one variable, and oftentimes it could be a change you need to make from within. Are you willing to make the necessary change?

I have converted the idea of a challenge to what I call a "new situation". When I am faced with a new situation, I ask myself, "What do I need to learn or contribute?" My belief and experiences have informed me that when I am presented with a challenge, especially one that I did not actively seek, it must be for a reason that will be beneficial to myself or others. Therefore, it is a moment to look within and derive the necessary strength and guidance to persevere.

You will know that you have been strengthened when you approach and face new situations with less apprehension, more ease, and the certainty that there is indeed a solution and a way forward.

Share your experiences with others, not because your challenges will be theirs or because you have the solution for their challenges. By sharing, you would have helped to ignite a spark that flames the belief for an individual's will to emerge and the capacity of the human spirit to become stronger from each new situation.

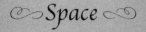

Space

Construct a space that is conducive for you.

Albeit your physical, psychological, emotional, or creative space, maintain a plan that enables you to adjust and remodel your space in order to minimize interferences or confusion to your personal signals.

Your space should not be created by happenstance. Examine your space to understand the knowledge and potential it holds, and the results it offers.

It is you that designs the plan to construct your space. To be most effective and reliable, have the vision and choice of how to construct your plan. Revisit and revise your plan as your journey provides new information. It must also be based on the knowledge of yourself and what you imagine and desire. To have knowledge, you must be aware and remain informed.

Each day can present new and different opportunities and challenges, which requires a constructive space that is beneficial for you to maneuver. Such a space is devoid of obstacles like fault, blame, fear, pride, jealousy, and envy. Work on minimizing or eradicating these obstacles from your space. Be willing to renovate and reconstruct a more resilient space. It is essential to design a plan devoid of hype and comparison.

Think of how to build a secure foundation as you remove hindrances, and seize opportunities to expand your foundation. Securing the foundation is a work in progress. As long as you are willing to reassess your construct and readjust as necessary, it will become easier to successfully venture and explore beyond your foundation.

Construct a space where you can think, grow, and increase your worth. Seek to create opportunities to include love, kindness, forgiveness, peace, and other attributes that will support positivity and strength. Within your space, remain keen and decisive when encountering new situations. Be astute to what will enrich as oppose to what could obstruct your life.

Do not diminish positive experiences with the negative ones. It is vital for us to celebrate our positive experiences and make a mental note of their contributing factors.

Understand why the positive experiences occurred in order to apply the factors, where applicable, in other situations.

Despite knowledge of your imperfections and limitations, I suggest here that your negative experiences can and should be used constructively to improve your space. Negative experiences call upon us to revisit our model and construction.

The more you fill your space with positivity— well-meaning people, ideas, and places and activities of interest— the more it will have little or no room for the other. So too, it will be able to withstand and recover easily from negative experiences.

Stand in your space and embrace yourself.

❧ Courage ❧

Courage is the willingness to act and experience the fullness of life's journey, regardless of what is expected or set upon you.

To exercise and build courage, you must remain awakened to moments or occasions when you consciously decide to stand on your values and beliefs, despite the outcome.

Courage is the readiness to decide that you will walk amongst the throng of naysayers and negativity without wavering in yourself and your convictions.

An essential knowledge to hold is that impediments and annoyances (whether tangible or abstract), in the face of courage, may delay your journey, but cannot deter.

Exercise courage amidst the slights of others and their misunderstandings of their limits. They exist only in a temporary space and can be impactful only if you validate their disposition towards you. The effects of hardships, minor or consequential, can be minimized or eliminated with courage.

It takes courage to understand that obstacles are placed in our paths to prevent us from side-stepping our better course and hence our purpose. Admittedly, other's life experiences may seem easier or more pleasurable, but can you know for sure when it is not your life?

Courage is the ability to truly look within and evaluate your options and possibilities. Courage is the decision to take the unpopular and necessary actions to lay foundations for outcomes you might not experience, but in which you believe will enhance society and the lives of others.

Have the courage to remain steadfast and committed to live in your experiences, without doubts— "what ifs" or "maybes". Forge ahead courageously and accept this experience of your life.

✑ Routine ✑

A routine provides certainty that gives order.

Although seamlessly unnoticed, human existence welcomes routine. A good example of the benefits of routines in our lives is the interconnectivity between humans and the natural world. It is undeniable that we are sustained by the order that nature provides.

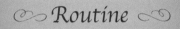

Although seldom spoken, often taken for granted, or even described as boredom, a routine can be relied upon as a contributor of ease. Such is the greeted repose to the otherwise bustle or fuss that creeps into life and becomes rooted as permanent distractions and, at times, sources of confusion.

A routine can serve as a welcomed ease to be experienced as a refuge and reinterpreted and normalized within our existence as a preserver of our energy.

Amongst the variables of life, we need to have a constant or two, and this is where the insertion of a routine contributes value to assist in normalizing the equation of life.

Regardless of how much you have going on in your life, I encourage you to arrange and create enjoyable activities and make a routine of experiencing these activities— whether on a daily, weekly, or monthly basis. You could start with one activity that will give you something to look forward to as a source of order in your life.

Routines in life can serve as an anchor, which holds us secure and steady to deal with the uncertainties that are often times arduous and beyond our control.

❧ *Disappointments* ❧

Disappointments are real but not lasting .

If you can recall the most heart wrenching disappointment you have experienced, unless it was most recent, chances are your memory of how you felt then and how you are feeling now are different.

If you are currently experiencing a disappointment, I can assure you that, in time, the impact will fade if you accurately assess why you are disappointed and what you need or are capable of doing to refresh your spirit.

To sort through the emotion of disappointment, I count missed opportunities, moments that slipped by, and unfulfilled desires amongst the broad categories of experiences that can evoke this emotion. I choose to see disappointments as life's small gentle elbows nudging us away from what we cannot see around the bend.

The point here is that disappointment can bring about a range of feelings, anywhere from irritation to hurt. And depending on how long it takes for us to realize that it appeared on our path for a reason and we need to change course or just pause, we will continue to experience the disappointment.

Use the time you need to recover from the reality of the disappointment. As you mollify your emotion, ponder what you have learned from the experience. What information or tools have you gathered from the process of placing the disappointment and the reason(s) for this very real emotion into its appropriate context?

If an experience should take you on a similar path, you might notice that you are better equipped to avert the same or similar disappointment. Also, you may now be ready to respond to similar circumstances without feeling disappointed.

✑ Change ✑

Change, although variable, is a constant in our lives.

Though you might not focus on the small or lesser changes of your day to day life, you are experiencing them. Whether you are actively participating in your transformation, change is simply a natural occurrence of our existence.

If you accede to this reality, you owe it to yourself to participate in the changes that surround and impact you.

Examine changes about and within you and determine how they correlate, accumulate, and aggregate within your life.

Become informed beyond the spoken or printed words. Ask yourself why and seek the answers that should resolve your inquiry. Educe new inquires that help bring about conversion within yourself and contribute to change around you.

Do not resist inevitable changes. Rather, strive to observe and understand so that you will have a hand and voice in the metamorphosis within and around you.

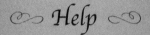

Help

The help you bestow is an offering for you.

When you are being helpful and expressing kindness of spirit in words or deeds, you will have no expectations of returns. When you genuinely help someone, the person should feel no sense of obligation from your words or disposition. And without a thought of the support you have given, you would have also helped yourself.

Helping without expectations nourishes and connects the human spirit. As we are connected through life, the help we bestow strengthens our individual spirit.

I encourage you to find someone who really needs your assistance and share a kind or thoughtful word. You do not need money or material items since you can give with your time, ideas, or a listening ear.

You will be uplifted and brightened when you allow yourself to see the joy or hear the silence in the spoken or unspoken thankfulness that your help evokes.

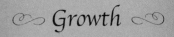
Growth

Grow from life's yeses, nos, and waits.

Although we have the right of choice, there is plenty about our beautiful and complex world that is beyond our control.

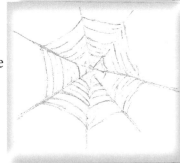

I encourage you to know when to try again or to be at ease with an outcome, as long as you have done all you could. In the process, do not compromise yourself or someone else, and be able to say, "That was my best."

It is also important to acknowledge, as part of your growth process, that others have the choice to respond from a vantage point of what they perceive to be their best decision. They can respond with a yes or no, with or without an explanation. I share this additional thought, which builds upon the first, as a caution to help you manage your expectations of others and situations that are outside your domain.

When you have worked to achieve a desired outcome and believe wholeheartedly it will bring you fulfillment, joy, and happiness, it is natural to anticipate a yes with pleasure. Know, however, upon receipt of the very yes you desired, you have the choice to say, "No thanks, I changed my mind," because circumstances have changed or your goals, wants or desires have shifted.

Seldom, however, it is as effortless to process an outcome of a no or have the ability to identify a wait when you have worked for a desired yes and envisioned what would follow. It may seem simple or is even natural and instinctive to easily accept the outcome of a no, try again, or just to wait.

However, it is the reality of how each of us receives and interprets unwelcoming and even disquieting responses that makes a difference in how we individually recover. Personal growth can be achieved from how we move forward from responses that are unexpected or true surprises.

There are several strategies to implement after an unexpected outcome. Whether you decide to try again, accept no, or have identified the decision as a wait, the strategy I recommend is for you to ask questions that will help you gain some insight. An attempt to understand how the decision was made and the factors that may have gone into the decision can help you better process the outcome and know how to embark on next steps. A thought to keep in mind, as well, is although it may be initially difficult, there are times when no or wait is the very best result you could receive.

I recall being told an initial no when I applied to my current job of over twenty years. I called the interviewer who would have been my supervisor and asked why I was not offered the position. From his silence, I sensed that he did not receive my question well or was taken by surprise that I asked.

However, I continued by explaining that it was the position I really wanted; I envisioned my contribution in this profession since I was four years old— yes really! I stated further that I knew I would do an outstanding job, and so I needed to know how I could improve or what I would need to do differently in the future since I was determined to try again.

As the phone call progressed, I deduced a more receptive listener, and although he was not to be credited for me receiving the very job a few weeks later, I had a very good working relationship with him as my supervisor. It is appropriate to openly thank my professor. Ultimately, it was my professor's recommendation that helped me to obtain the second interview, which secured the job I have enjoyed practicing.

The desire to know why you are told no can evoke a line of inquiry that could help you better prepare in the future for the same job, another job, or a totally different situation in other areas of your life. Whenever you are told no, try asking, "Why?" Be prepared to receive the response, assess it, and decide if it is the time to try again or if this was an experience for you to gain more insight and grow. Keep in mind that the person or persons also have a choice and hence the option of responding again with no.

As I developed within my profession, I took opportunities to advance in multiple areas, expanded my knowledge, and prepared myself for other prospects. Through these plans and the ambition to advance, there came about a different position I desired, and so I decided to apply. I was well prepared and knew I would have brought about positive changes within the group. Overall, I would have done an excellent job for the organization.

Not long after I submitted that application, instinctively I made the decision that I would use the interviewing process to discover how the panel (collectively and individually) would respond to someone who would not give the expected answers. This was a risk I was willing to take. As important as it was for me to advance in my profession, it was even more important that my experiences and contributions would be made amongst people who could appreciate my honest and unique input.

Also, I knew even before the outcome that I would not try again for this particular position if the outcome was no. Within myself, there was a sense of anticipated acceptance that whatever the outcome, it would be good for me.

When I received the call, the answer was no. Here again I inquired why, for the purpose of knowing and understanding. Also, I had prepared myself to objectively listen to the answers. Listening to the responses was rather distressing, not because of the no, but the explanations were meritless and fabricated.

However, the inquiry affirmed much about myself and taught me what I needed to know about the totality of the decision and the surrounding situations. I confirmed what my intuition had communicated to me— it was a good outcome. That path would have been unsuitable for me.

My transition from desiring the position to acceptance of the no, despite the surrounding circumstances, was remarkably seamless because I was prepared to learn and grow.

When I reflect, I am sure of what I may have surmised then, I am blissfully pleased and have been thankful for that no. The decision saved me from what would have been stifling shenanigans that would have attempted to evaporate my energy without appreciation.

The outcome of the no allowed me to recalibrate and reset my focus. I also know that my preparation was not lost. Since then, I have increased my skills and created several opportunities that have been rewarding for my team, organization, and self. The value of that response has never been lost to me. My path brought me along to meet and work with energetic and positive people, which has allowed me to affirm the value of a no.

It is also important to say, "thank you", when it is deserved. So, "thank you" to my colleagues with whom I enjoy working, a senior manager who acknowledged my work and endorsed a subsequent promotion, and a supervisor who has always given my work fair assessments.

A response of a no gives us time to reconsider our thoughts and strategies. Each time you prepare yourself for one venture or an opportunity to contribute and implement your ideas, and you are told no, do not be dismayed. You are being prepared for different prospects. Each practice should be accepted as training for your crescendo moments.

Do not exhaust your energy. Do not force against life.

There are times when you can try again and convert a no to a yes. Also, there will be other times when it is just not worth the effort to try for a particular yes.

A response of wait sometimes can be mistaken for no. For each of us, we must endeavor to know the differences between a no and a wait. While we wait, there is much we can do. During the time of waiting, we can learn to be patient. It is in this period, we can think and create. Be imaginative and plan what you will do if the answer converts to a yes. This waiting period will help you appreciate the eventual yes.

Be thankful when you receive a yes— whether it is after your first or several tries, a period of waiting, or a no. Just be thankful and make the totality of the experience remain indelible. This could be an experience you will need in the future to reflect upon and revisit to gain insight or strength. And regardless of the context, when you receive something you have worked for and desired, appreciate the opportunity.

Seek ways to invest in each yes you receive, assess each no, and when there is a waiting period, take the time to prepare for your yes that may come. Also, the growth you achieve in one area is often transferable to other areas of your life.

In this journey of life, yeses, nos, and waits are equally important. In all three of these alternatives, you must stay in your lane, focus on what you know about yourself, live your purpose, and conserve your energy. Our beautiful and complex world will appear simpler and your appreciation for its beauty will flourish.

❦ *You* ❧

Take a moment for you!

Everything that makes you
different is what makes
you special.

Exercise your options,
and give yourself the
permission
to be unequivocally
You!

About the Author

As a child, I really enjoyed the art of conversation and especially with older people. I enjoyed their stories about growing up and what the world was like when they were young. I used to have long conversations with my father who encouraged my voice, nurtured my spirit, and supported my directness. I lost my mother early in life; however, her life lessons to me and for me have been enduring. It is also important to share that my strengths and limitations were cradled by several members of my extended family, especially Mimi.

Now that I am older, I continue to enjoy my elders and share ideas, thoughts, and lessons with younger people. I have practiced law for over twenty years. I appreciate my practice and the contributions my work provides for people and the environment. My practice of law is supported by my knowledge of the natural sciences, economics and finance, and international business transactions. As I continue to make positive differences to the environment, I genuinely want to help people identify and operate from their "best self".

For over twenty years, I have mentored children, young people, and adults from across the globe. Even as a child, I was insightful and understood well people's emotions. I recall being very helpful with ideas and had the readiness to find solutions. From these experiences, I decided that life-coaching, which goes beyond mentoring, is an area that is compatible with my expertise and passion. With this awareness, I expanded my career portfolio into the area of life-coaching, and continue to extend my network and contribution globally as a *certified life coach*.

On a personal level, I have known my husband for more than forty years; we are friends and still laugh at each other's jokes! We have been blessed with two children who are giving and helpful to others and have made positive life choices for themselves and communities. I am happy to share that I get along with people of all cultures and view the world as my home.

I have great joy when I share life experiences and lessons with my daughter, nephew, son, and husband. I enjoy decorating my home, cooking, baking, entertaining, and watching period films with my daughter. Unwavering, has been my appreciation for classical music, books, and fabric!

I welcome your thoughts and feedback, with the hope that your read of this book will be helpful, and you will continue this conversation with me. You may contact me directly at: memzabeth@gmail.com.

Also, visit www.globalves.com to find more of my books and other VES books.

Another book by this author:

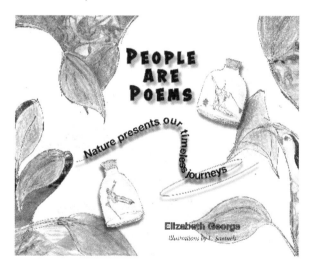